IMAGES OF WAR

GERMAN ARMY ON THE EASTERN FRONT
THE RETREAT 1943 – 1945

RARE PHOTOGRAPHS FROM WARTIME ARCHIVES

IAN BAXTER

Pen & Sword
MILITARY

First published in this format in Great Britain in 2016 by
PEN AND SWORD MILITARY
An imprint of
Pen & Sword Books Ltd
47 Church Street, Barnsley
South Yorkshire
S70 2AS

ISBN 978 1 47382 267 2

A CIP catalogue record for this book is available from the British Library

Printed and bound in England
By CPI Group (UK) Ltd, Croydon, CR0 4YY

Pen & Sword Books Ltd incorporates the Imprints of Pen & Sword Aviation,
Pen & Sword Family History, Pen & Sword Maritime, Pen & Sword Military,
Pen & Sword Discovery, Pen & Sword Politics, Pen & Sword Atlas,
Pen & Sword Archaeology, Wharncliffe Local History, Leo Cooper,
Wharncliffe True Crime, Wharncliffe Transport, Pen & Sword Select,
Pen & Sword Military Classics, The Praetorian Press, Claymore Press,
Remember When, Seaforth Publishing and Frontline Publishing

For a complete list of Pen & Sword titles please contact
PEN & SWORD BOOKS LIMITED
47 Church Street, Barnsley, South Yorkshire, S70 2AS, England
E-mail: enquiries@pen-and-sword.co.uk
Website: www.pen-and-sword.co.uk

Contents

Chapter 1
Summer & Winter Battles 1943

In July 1943, the German Army launched what proved to be its last great offensive on the Eastern Front – against the Kursk salient. Despite massive losses sustained by their forces at Stalingrad, which led to the subsequent destruction of the 6th Army, Hitler was determined as ever not to give up the fight in Russia. It was here at Kursk that the Führer was confronted with a very tempting strategic opportunity that he was convinced could yield him victory. Within the huge salient, measuring some 120 miles wide and 75 miles deep, he tried to persuade his generals that his forces could attack from the north and south of the salient in a huge pincer movement and encircle the Red Army. In Hitler's view, the offensive, codenamed 'Zitadelle', would be the greatest armoured battle ever won by both the German Army and Waffen-SS. As with the opening phases of 'Barbarossa' in June 1941, a confident Hitler had predicted that 'he only had to kick in the front door and the whole rotten edifice would come crashing down.' Despite Hitler's confidence, the German generals were not blind to the great difficulties facing them at Kursk. In fact, a number of them were concerned at the enemy's growing strength. Intelligence had already confirmed that the Red Army had constructed a number of major defensive belts, each of which were subdivided into two or even three layers of almost impregnable strongholds. Although there were no accurate figures, these Soviet belts were some 150 miles deep. Each belt consisted of many anti-tank strong points and an extensive network of obstacles with a maze of intricate blockhouses and trenches. The Russian soldiers that were dug-in along these belts were well camouflaged and heavily armed with plenty of provisions to sustain them during long contact with the enemy. For three long months the Red Army had been prepared for the German attack. Improved intelligence had allowed Russian commanders to predict exactly the strategic focal point of the German attack. It was this combined collection of battlefield intelligence that proved that 'Zitadelle' was doomed to failure even before it had begun. The German Army were determined to rejuvenate their Blitzkrieg tactics, but the immense preparations that had gone into constructing the Soviet defences meant that the Germans were never going to succeed in penetrating deeply into the Red Army fortifications.

The battle of the Kursk was probably the first modern Soviet operation of the war. Despite the fact that the Red Army lacked the technological superiority of individual weapons, they had a well-prepared defensive programme, which included elaborate deception plans to confuse the enemy.

During the early morning of 5 July 1943, the long awaited battle began in earnest with the Germans unleashing one of their largest artillery bombardments of the war. In fact, the bombardment was so intense that in no less than one hour the Germans had hurled more shells than they had used in both Poland and the Western Campaign put together. Once the bombardments had subsided German ground attacks were ordered forward into action. Their objective was to break through the Kursk-Orel highway and railway and then drive southwards to Kursk. In order to reduce the vulnerability of the armoured vehicles that were to achieve this ambitious advance, General Walter Model, commander of the 9th Army, insisted that dismounted infantry accompany his armoured vehicles. Although Model's tactics helped reduce tank losses on the first morning, it was at the expense of massive infantry casualties. During the rest of the first day the German 9th Army fell far short of its objectives, due to the fact that the Soviet Central Front had correctly anticipated the attack sector. Attacking on a 25-mile-wide front, the Germans found themselves trapped in the huge defensive minefields, and desperately called upon engineering units to clear them under artillery fire. Although engineering units were able to clear some of the mines, they were generally unsuccessful. As a consequence German losses in the Soviet minefields were massive.

All over the German northern front troops tried their best to push forward under relentless Russian fire. To the German soldier in this battle, it was unlike any other engagement they had previously encountered. The Russians constantly strengthened their defences through reinforcement, skilfully deploying mobile armour and anti-tank reserves to compensate for their high losses.

Within twenty-four hours of the initial attack the 9th Army's 25-mile front had been reduced to some 20 miles. By 7 July this dropped to around 8 miles wide, and the following day only less than a mile. Not only had the front shrunk, but the depth of the German attack had been significantly reduced. By 10 July, through sheer weight of Soviet strength and stubborn combat, German mobile units of the 9th Army were finally forced to a standstill and were fighting for their lives. Everything that could go wrong for the German 9th Army had been played out on the blood-soaked plains of Kursk.

After a week of the attack the German Army had only moved some eight miles. On 12 July this prompted the Red Army to launch their offensive against the 2nd Army at Orel. With all their might they began to pulverise the German positions into the ground. The 9th Army were now compelled to withdraw or face total annihilation. Human casualties were huge, as were losses in equipment. The German Panzer divisions had lost some 300 of their trusted Pz.Kpfw.III & IVs, half a dozen Tiger Is and 50 tank destroyers.

While the northern front was continuously hampered by strong enemy resistance, in the south of the salient the Voronezh Front fared less well against the German Army and its elite SS counterparts of the II SS Panzer Corps. These units of Army Group South were very powerful and consisted of an immense phalanx of armour. One of the most powerful armoured forces consisted of Hoth's 4th Panzer Army. This armoured force had achieved remarkable progress on the first day of the attack and had successfully forced its way forward through strong Russian defences. By 6 July it had smashed its way through Red Army lines and radioed that the advanced elements were some nine miles beyond their start lines. Along the rest of the southern front other German forces were making equally good progress against the Red Army. But as in the north, attack frontages and penetration depth were reduced as the attack proceeded. Consequently within three days the front had been reduced from a 16 mile front to 1½ miles. Yet again the Russians had heroically held their positions to the last man. The many thousands of mines and artillery pieces were again successful in delaying the German attack and inflicting appalling losses on the Germans. Across threatened sectors of the front where German forces seemed to penetrate areas more deeply the Russians quickly brought up additional stocks of mines. Over 90,000 of these mines alone were laid during the battle by small mobile groups of engineers at night. Once again the Germans fell victim to the mines. Within five days of heavy fighting many German units had lost immeasurable amounts of men and equipment. The elite Großdeutschland Division for instance, which began the battle with 118 tanks, only had 3 Tigers, 6 Panthers, and 11 Pz.Kpfw.III and IV tanks left operational. The XLVIII Panzer Corps reported, overall, 38 Panthers operational with 131 awaiting repair, out of the 200 it started with on 5 July.

By 12 July the Red Army had finally ground down the German Army at Kursk and threw its offensive timetable off schedule. For the first time in the war the Soviets had savagely contested every foot of ground and were finally on an equal footing. The German offensive at Kursk had dealt them a severe battering from which they were never to properly recover. They had lost some thirty divisions, including seven Panzer divisions. According to official Soviet sources, as many as 49,822 German troops were killed or missing. They had lost a staggering 1,614 tanks and self-propelled guns that were committed to action. As for the Red Army, they suffered much higher losses with some 177,847 being killed and injured. They lost 2,586 Soviet tanks and self-propelled guns during the operation. The battle of Kursk had finally ended the myth of German invincibility and was the first time that the blitzkrieg concept had failed. As for the German Army the tide had finally turned. They lost the initiative in the east and now began a fighting withdrawal.

Following the catastrophe at Kursk, German warfare was now on the defensive. But in spite of the failure, the German High Command still clung to the view that fighting there had squeezed all available resources out of the Red Army. They ardently believed that the rest of the summer campaign could be devoted to a series of tactical solutions that could straighten out the front and prepare its defences for the onset of the winter. The German soldier now believed that he belonged to the weaker army and had to accept that offensive and defensive operations had to be altered with the seasons. To the soldier this undoubtedly prolonged the agony of fighting on the Eastern Front. Indeed, throughout the whole summer of 1943 the German Army had suffered permanent change. It had lost its courage and the will to advance. Hope was tainted by the growing prospect of being sucked into another bloody protracted battle and being cut-off and literally annihilated by its giant foe. With nothing but a string of defeats in its wake the German Army reluctantly withdrew across Russia. In southern Russia a number of advanced units of Army Group South tried their best to hold onto vital areas of ground in order to contain the overly-extended front. By the end of July 1943 Army Group South had a total of 822,000 troops opposing an estimated 1,710,000 Russians. The army group had 1,161 tanks, about half of them operational, while the

Russians had 2,872 tanks. Here in the south the majority of the units were seriously under strength and still further depleted by vehicles constantly being taken out for repair. This undoubtedly left a substantial lack of armour to support the troops on the front lines. Consequently Army Group South was finally forced to withdraw, while avoiding being cut off and suffering the same fate as that of the 6th Army at Stalingrad. At the end of July a substantial amount of men and equipment had withdrawn into the Donetz area.

Further north, in the middle sector of the Eastern Front, Army Group Centre were trying desperately to hold the Red Army from breaking through their lines. But their strength too had been severely weakened by the battle of Kursk. By 5 August the Russians captured Orel. Simultaneous drives along the southern sector of the front saw the Red Army take Kharkov, the most fought-over city in Russia. Soviet troops then pressed forward and crossed the Donetz. These powerful drives soon threatened to envelop General Kleist's Army Group A, which was still bitterly contesting every foot of ground in the Crimea. It seemed that large parts of the German southern front would soon be overrun, but on 31 August Hitler reluctantly ordered further withdrawals. The Hitler 'Order' averted a catastrophe, but it only temporarily stabilised the front. Already Army Group Centre had been pierced in three places and the whole sector in that part of the Eastern Front begun to disintegrate under the sheer weight of the Red Army. By 8 September advanced Russian units were reported to be no less than thirty miles from the Dnieper and by 14 September were threatening the city of Kiev. On 15 September Hitler once again ordered another withdrawal; this time his forces were to be moved back to the line of the Dnieper, Sozh and Pronya rivers, approximately the line reached by the German Army during their victorious 'Barbarossa' campaign in July 1941. However, the instruction to permit an ordered withdrawal came too late. What followed was thousands of German soldiers frantically racing for the river positions, with Red Army troops smashing onto a number of formations and totally annihilating them. By 30 September the Russians had five bridgeheads over the Dnieper.

For the German Army on the Eastern Front the summer campaign of 1943 had been completely disastrous. During five weeks of almost continuous bloody fighting it had withdrawn some 150 miles along a 650-mile front. While these forces retreated Hitler had decreed a 'scorched earth policy', in which all main roads, railway lines, power stations, farms and factories were to be destroyed. However, in all the panic and confusion, the demolition teams did not have enough time to implement the destruction of the main roads which the Red Army used for its main advance. As the winter of 1943/44 reared its head, during October a feeling of further despair and gloom prevailed in the German Army. To the depressed soldiers who had to endure the third Russian winter a dull conviction quickly gripped them that the war in the East was lost — yet without any sight of its end. The German Army was still dug deep into the heartlands of Soviet Russia. But unlike 1941 and 1942, they had lost the initiative.

Slowly the German soldier retreated across a bleak and hostile landscape, always outnumbered, and constantly low on fuel, ammunition and other desperately-needed supplies. In three months following the defeat at Kursk, Army Group South only received some 32,000 replacements, although it had suffered more than 130,000 casualties. The equipment situation too continued to decline, especially in Panzer units.

The whole of the German Army in the east was thus faced with a more dangerous prospect than ever before. To make matters worse, an anti-partisan conflict added yet another dimension to the war in Russia. With word of the advancing Red Army, Ukrainian nationalist partisans, Polish underground groups and communist partisans began raiding German outposts, barracks, police stations, rail depots, supply dumps, and ambushing convoys and trains. As the German troops withdrew they had to clear out the partisans before they became prey to the snipers and saboteurs. All this, and continuous pressure from Hitler to defend every yard of land with their blood, made fighting ever more inhumane. For the German Army the closing months of 1943 passed, like the autumn, in a sequence of bitter bloodthirsty battles, which consequently sapped the will and energy of German soldier almost beyond repair.

German troops survey the damage to a Russian artillery position in the early summer of 1943. By this period of the war much of the German front was either stagnated or cracking under the sheer weight of Russian opposition.

On the central front, German soldiers can be seen preparing cover along the front utilising straw to camouflage their position. While many parts of the front in early 1943 stagnated, in the south and in the Ukraine, operations were being undertaken. The German Army, in spite of losing Stalingrad, had yet again demonstrated its renowned powers of recovery.

German troops cross a river in a rubber boat somewhere in southern Russia in 1943. Although after the loss of Stalingrad the Germans managed to stablise the Eastern Front from further destruction, its soldiers no longer had the strength to mount another successful offensive like those seen in 1941 and 1942.

During the opening phase of the Kursk offensive and a 7.5cr le.IG.18 artillery crew can be seen the moment the gun is fire against an enemy target. Note the gunner plugging his ear

A soldier poses for the camera with a 7.5cm le.IG.18. These small robust artillery pieces were highly mobile, and were often vital for supporting infantry during offensive and defensive actions.

A German artillery position opens fire during a night time artillery bombardment of Soviet positions. In the summer of 1943, the German Army were determined to rejuvenate their Blitzkrieg tactics, but the immense preparations that had gone into constructing the Soviet defences meant that the Germans were never going to succeed in penetrating into the strategic depths of the Red Army fortifications.

An MG34 machine gun position with machine gunner and feeder seen in action against an enemy target. By this period of the war German infantry divisions had been severely mauled. A number had suffered serious losses, but could be re-equipped without withdrawing them completely from combat.

German troops with their commanding officer on the front during the summer of 1943. Two of the soldiers are wearing the splinter-pattern German Army camouflage used on heavy reversible winter uniforms.

German infantry crew with a rubber boat after disembarking from a river. The soldiers are wearing a full complement of kit and armed with their bolt action Kar98K rifles, the standard German infantry weapon issued to the soldiers throughout the war.

A 5cm light 36 model mortar crew in action. During the war the mortar became the standard infantry support weapon giving the soldier valuable high explosive capability beyond the range of rifles and grenades.

An MG34 machine gunner dug in a position somewhere along the Eastern Front. This weapon appears attached to a Lafette 34 sustained fire mount. Each infantry battalion contained an MG company fielding eight MG34 machine guns on the sustained fire mount. A heavy machine gun squad often consisted of six men.

Three photographs showing German infantry on the retreat. To the German soldier the prolonged agony of fighting on the Eastern Front further magnified with every setback. Hope was tainted by the growing prospect of being sucked into another bloody protracted battle, being cut off and literally annihilated by its giant foe.

Soldiers in a typical dugout during defensive actions in southern Russia. Many parts of the German front were trying desperately to hold the Red Army from breaking through their lines.

An **MG42** machine gun on an attached Lafette sustained fire mount with optical sight. Note the special pads on the front of the tripod. These were specially used when the weapon was being moved on the carrier's back and would allow the gunner some reasonable degree of comfort.

Infantry are seen crossing a makeshift wooden bridge in order to move soldiers and light ordnance across the river.

Three photographs showing an infantry mortar crew with their 8cm sGrW 34 mortar. The design of this weapon was conventional and could be broken down for transportation into three loads (barrel, bipod and base plate). It gained a reputation for extreme accuracy and rapid fire rate.

A heavy MG34 machine gun crew in a defensive position. The MG34 has been attached to a Lafette 34 sustained-fire mount with optical sight.

German troops can be seen crossing a bridge. It was imperative throughout the war that pioneers built bridges as quickly and effectively as possible without hindering units up front that were fighting. Keeping frontline units re-supplied was a constant logistical nightmare for the Wehrmacht, and it often resulted in leading units grinding to a halt until additional supplies were brought up.

In a shallow dugout in an open field, infantry can be seen armed with their standard armament – the Karabiner 98K bolt action rifle – preparing to move forward into action. When in line normally two battalions would be forward and one in reserve. However, due to the front line being overstretched it was not uncommon to have all three on the front.

Infantry rest and tuck into their rations from their dugout during defensive actions in 1943. Throughout the second half of 1943 the German Army was compelled to fight and defend its position to the bitter end. In spite of the mounting casualties Hitler still prohibited all voluntary withdrawals.

Wehrmacht troops rest before resuming operations. With the disintegration of the Panzerwaffe in Army Group Centre during the summer of 1943, staunch German defence was now required in order to contain the Red Army and thus prevent it from continuing its advance and reaching the borders of the Reich.

An 8cm sGrW 34 mortar crew during a fire mission. Each battalion fielded some six of these excellent 8cm sGrW 34 mortars, which could fire fifteen projectiles per minute to a range of 2,625 yards. Aside from high-explosive and smoke bombs, this weapon also fired a 'bounding' bomb. It was very common for infantry, especially during intensive long periods of action, to fire their mortar from either trenches or dug-in positions where the mortar crew could also be protected from enemy fire.

A light MG34 machine gun crew inside a building during urbanised fighting. In built-up areas the crews often had to operate forward with the rifle platoons and in light machine gun roles with bipods only – as in this photograph. They were still able sometimes to take advantage of the situation and revert back to a heavy machine gun role.

Three photographs showing Wehrmacht troops during a decoration ceremony. These decoration ceremonies were signs of honour and distinction, and were also a way for the Nazi leadership to bolster morale, highlighting their men's individual bravery and leadership out in the field. However, out on the battlefield these much decorated soldiers became obvious targets to enemy snipers.

A Panzerman dressed in his famili[ar] black panzer uniform confers with an assault gunner wearing his special field grey uniform worn by tank destroyer and self propelled assault gun units.

A photograph showing the 2cm flak 38 quadruple mount. This gun could unleash a hurricane of fire and was able to discharge 1,800 rounds per minute from all four o[f] its barrels. This weapon had two operators, one who fired the top left and bottom right guns, while the other fired the top right and bottom left guns. The loader coul[d] quickly change the magazines while the other continued to fire. Each of these flak guns had a practical rate of fire of 120 round[s] per minute, with a maximum horizontal range of 4,800 metres.

Out in a field an 8.8cm flak gun being readied by its crew for action. This was the most famous German anti-aircraft gun of the Second World War, and in this photograph the barrel has been lowered to be used in an anti-tank role. The gun is bolted on a cruciform platform from which it fired with outriggers extended. Note expended shells laying about the position.

In a shallow dugout in a field an MG34 machine gun crew can be seen. Both wear the waterproof Zeltbahn, and can be seen armed with the MG34 machine gun on its bipod, M1924 stick grenade and a 98K bolt action rifle.

As German troops withdraw from their positions they are ordered to burn and destroy everything in their wake, known as the 'Scorched Earth Policy'. Here soldiers armed with their standard army issue bolt action rifles stand near a burning farmstead during its unit's retreat in the late summer of 1943.

A German soldier armed with his standard army issue 98K bolt action rifle stands guard over a group of Soviet PoWs. Their fate can only be imagined, during this period of the war.

During what probably is a decoration ceremony out in the field in late 1943, soldiers are seen in file standing behind a 7.5cm le.IG18 gun. These small light highly mobile infantry guns were more than capable of providing troops with vital offensive and defensive fire support, particularly when heavy artillery was unavailable.

German troops seen in a village. An abandoned Soviet artillery piece can be seen on tow. In spite of the German withdrawal in 1943, there were a number of areas along the front where the Germans actually regained ground, often leaving the Russians fleeing for their lives and abandoning weaponry.

An 8cm Gr. W34 mortar position. During the war the mortar had become the standard infantry support weapon, giving the soldier valuable high explosive capability beyond the range of rifles or grenades. Yet one of the major drawbacks was its accuracy. Even with an experienced mortar crew, it generally required ten bombs to achieve a direct hit on one single target.

An interesting photograph showing what appears to be an abandoned Nebelwerfer 41 position. The Nebelwerfer was a German multiple rocket launcher and served with units of the Nebeltruppen. A later version, the Nebelwerfer 42, comprised of five rocket tubes.

An MG34 machine gun mounted on a tripod being used in an anti-aircraft role. The machine gun position has been well sited inside a defensive position. This machine gun crew probably belongs to an artillery regiment.

In a forward observation post a soldier can be seen looking through a pair of scissor binoculars. Although observers were primarily tasked with detecting targets, they also looked for weapon muzzles, moving infantry, armoured vehicles, fires, smoke from cooking and anything else they could detect to locate their enemy. From this position the observer could send details of enemy movements back to divisional headquarters.

A battery troop along a road. Note the condition of the road and how the animal cart is struggling through the mud. Mud was a constant hindrance to both animal draught and wheeled vehicles on the Eastern Front and often held up entire divisions, sometimes for days.

Wearing a greatcoat and fur hat this soldier is more than likely a troop leader as he is armed with the 9mm MP38 or MP40 machine pistol. The MP38/40 machine pistol was commonly called the 'Schmeisser'.

During an urbanised action an anti-tank crew prepares to fire a projectile from a PaK35/36 anti-tank gun. The PaK35/36 was the standard anti-tank gun of the German Army during the early part of the war, and was still used until 1945. It weighed only 432kg and had a sloping splinter shield. The gun fired a solid shot round at a muzzle velocity of 762m/s (2,500ft/s) to a maximum range of 4,025m.

Infantrymen wearing the standard Army greatcoat are assembled in the snow posing for the camera. They appear to be in a forward defensive position comprising a trench system and various dugouts.

An 8cm Granatwerfer GrW34 mortar and crew in a dugout position. There was a platoon of four 8cm mortars assigned to a grenadier battalion's machine gun company. The Germans found the mortar so effective that they often used captured Soviet mortars and fired their own ammunition from them using German firing tables.

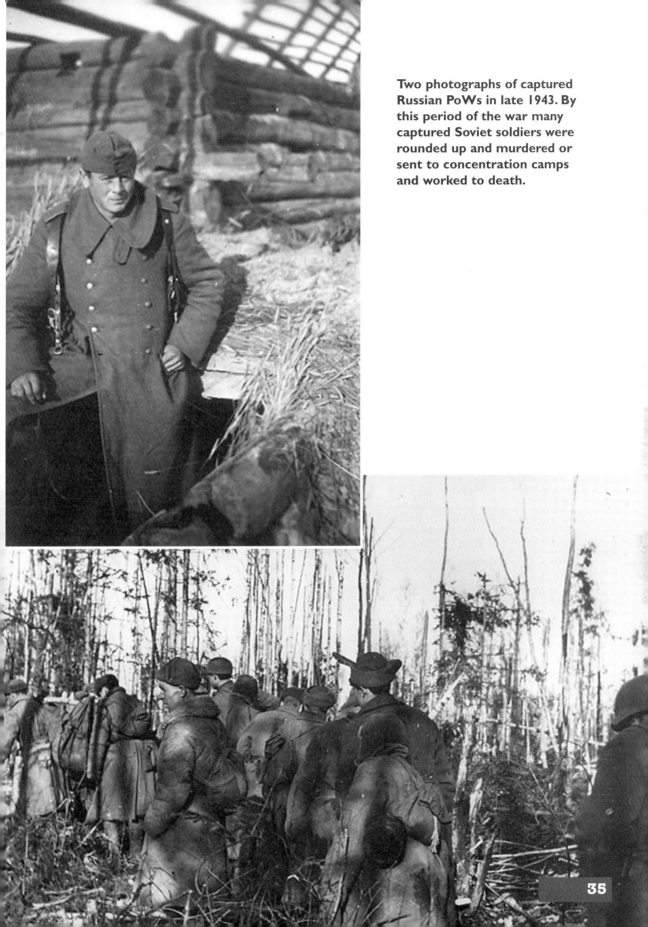

Two photographs of captured Russian PoWs in late 1943. By this period of the war many captured Soviet soldiers were rounded up and murdered or sent to concentration camps and worked to death.

A supply vehicle has halted in the snow during winter operations in late 1943. Throughout the war on the Eastern Front the supply situation was exacerbated by the almost non-existence of proper roads throughout the Soviet Union. Halftracks and other tracked vehicles were utilised to help speed up the supply of ammunition and other equipment desperately required for the front as many wheeled vehicles struggled in the arctic conditions.

A light MG34 machine gunner wearing his standard army issue greatcoat and a fur cap. With the bipod extended and the belt loaded, the machine gunner could effectively move the weapon quickly from one position to another, or throw it to the ground and put it into operation, with deadly effect.

Captured Russian booty including discarded helmets, rifles, machine guns and communication cable reels are sprawled across a position. Note the defensive dugouts. These dugouts often comprised of elaborate underground tunnels where soldiers sometimes lived for months.

German soldiers examine what appears to be the destroyed remains of a Soviet tank.

Chapter 2
Winter Warfare
1944

The military situation on the Eastern Front in January 1944 was dire for the German Army. It had entered into the New Year with a dwindling number of soldiers to man the battle lines. Hitler's reluctance to concede territory was still proving to be very problematic for commanders in the field. In spite of the worsening condition of the German Army, the soldiers were compelled to fight on. The persistent lack of strategic direction in the east was causing major trouble too. The Red Army, however, was now in greater strength than ever before.

In Army Group North, General George von Kuechler's force had been for some weeks trying in vain to hold its positions along its northern defences against strong Russian forces. From the Volkhov River to the Gulf of Finland the front was covered with a string of trenches and shell holes, reminiscent of trench warfare during the First World War. By 15 January 1944, the defences were finally attacked by three Soviet fronts, the Leningrad, Volkhov and Second Baltic. The 18th Army, which bore the brunt of the main attacks, were outnumbered by at least 3:1 in divisions. As usual the German troops were expected to hold the front, but the overwhelming enemy firepower proved too much and Kuechler's Army Group was compelled to fall back under a hurricane of enemy fire. Within four days of the attack the Russians had successfully breached Army Group North's defences in three places. This effectively wrenched open a huge corridor allowing Red Army troops to pour through towards the besieged city of Leningrad. Troops of the German 18th Army were beginning to disintegrate. Already it had incurred 40,000 casualties trying to contain the Soviets. Fighting in the mud and freezing water, the men were totally exhausted and unable to hold back the enemy for any appreciable length of time. Hitler on the other hand still prohibited all voluntary withdrawals and reserved all decisions to withdraw to himself. In a leadership conference held by the Führer the commanders were told to infuse determination in their men and to strengthen faith in ultimate victory. But in spite of Hitler's measures, the German Army were unable to stem the rout of the advancing Russian forces. By 26 January the city of Leningrad was liberated after nine hundred days of siege. The 18th Army was now split into three parts and struggled to hold a front forward of the Luga River. The entire German northern front was now beginning to crumble and Hitler openly blamed Kuechler for its failure. On 1 February 1944 the General was relieved of his command and temporarily replaced by Hitler's Eastern Front 'trouble shooter', General Walther Model. Model was a great improviser who was quite capable of changing the tactical situation in Army Group North. Almost immediately Model went to work by introducing his 'Schild und Schwert' (Shield and Sword) policy, which stated that no soldiers were to withdraw without his express permission, unless they paved the way for a counterstroke later. Along the front both the 16th and 18th Armies, which were badly depleted with only the 12th Panzer and 58th Infantry divisions intact, were ordered to hold the line on the Luga River, east of a series of hastily constructed defences known as the Panther Line. Model, determined at all costs to prevent the front degenerating into a panic flight, collected stragglers and sent them back to the line. He cancelled leaves, sent walking wounded to their units, and sent a number of the rear-echelon troops to the front. Without hesitation he requested more reinforcements, which included Waffen-SS replacements, naval coastal batteries and Luftwaffe troops.

Throughout February morale was temporarily restored to the frontline units. As the German forces stepped back to defend the Panther Line they had gained just enough strength to hold back the Red Army. During March the Russians began exerting more pressure, especially against the 16th Army that was defending positions along the Baltic, but the spring thaw had arrived early and melting snow had turned the roads on which the Russians were travelling into quagmires. The conditions were so bad that forward units from the 16th Army reported that Soviet tanks could be seen sinking up to their turrets in mud. It seemed the Panther Line was holding, with the weather playing a major part in containing the Red Army. Now it would not be until the early summer that the Red Army would resume its push. Army Group North was now stabilised.

This was a major success for Model, which now earned him a new command in Army Group South. On 30 March 1944, less than a week before Army Group South was re-designated Army Group North Ukraine, Model replaced Manstein and was installed as Commander-in-Chief.

For three long months Army Group South had fought a series of bitter and bloody battles in order to stem the gradual deterioration of its forces in southern Russia. Conditions for the German Army between January and March 1944 were dismal. Supplies were inadequate, and replacements in men were far below what was needed to sustain all its divisions along the front. To make matters worse, in early January a 110-mile breach between Army Group Centre and Army Group South had developed. Neither army group had sufficient forces to plug the gap, and by the end of the month, when the Belorussian Front pushed the 2nd Army to the line of the Ipa River the gap opened even wider.

For the next few weeks, further pressure was applied on Army Group South. By this time the German front was disintegrating under persistent overwhelming enemy attacks. German mobile reserves had all been worn down almost to extinction and this led to a number of units being encircled. One of the largest pockets to develop was in the Kovel-Korsun area of the lower Dnieper where seven German divisions and the 5th SS Wiking Division were trapped. By using some of the last Panzers in the area, Manstein managed to drive a wedge and create a corridor for the encircled men, and held it open to allow them to escape. The remnants of the shattered divisions that successfully broke out struggled southeast under continuous Russian fire. To the north of Kovel-Korsun the situation for the rest of Manstein's Army Group was equally dire. The bulk of the men were totally exhausted. The worn out 1st and 4th Panzer armies were all that were left to support troop operations in the south, and they were being slowly compressed against the Carpathian Mountains. By early March advanced Soviet units had reached the outskirts of the city of Tarnopol. Within days of their arrival Red Army troops advanced through the ravaged city but were soon beaten back by strong German defences. As German soldiers fought for Tarnopol Hitler issued another Führer Order appealing for his forces on the Eastern Front to use towns, cities and surrounding areas as fortified positions in order to slow the Soviet drive westward. In other words he was calling upon every soldier to hold to the last man. Many soldiers that were given the awesome task of defending these towns and cities nicknamed these suicidal assignments 'Himmelfahrts-Kommandos' ('missions to Heaven'). In total, Hitler designated some twenty-six cities and larger towns on still-occupied Soviet territory as fortified positions; among those in the south were Tarnopol, Proskurov, Kovel, Brody, Vinnitsa, and Pervomaysk.

In the city of Tarnopol conditions for the troops were appalling. For days they held out inside the ruins while being subjected to sustained bombardments from heavy Soviet artillery. By 21 March, the Red Army had amassed enough strength to mount an attack on the front between Tarnopol and Proskurov. With one single blow 200 tanks of the 1st and 4th Tank Armies smashed through the German defensive line, consisting mainly of the 68th Infantry and 7th Panzer Divisions, carrying them along like driftwood. Two days later a force of the Russian 1st Tank Army wheeled west with all its might and hammered its way through bewildered German infantry divisions that were defending Tarnopol. Those troops that were defending surrounding areas were thrown back some ten miles, leaving behind a garrison inside the doomed city. Some of the defenders of Tarnopol reported that the scenes were reminiscent of Stalingrad. For the next three weeks the 4,000 strong garrison held out. When a rescue operation by the 9th SS Panzer Division tried to relieve the trapped force during the night of April 15/16, only fifty-three men managed to break out and reach the German lines; the rest were captured or killed.

In spite of the horrifying casualties and huge losses of equipment inflicted upon Army Group South, its forces as a whole during the winter of 1944 had generally defended its positions relatively well against terrible odds. In fact in some places it even held the line. When Model replaced Manstein at the end of March the crisis in the south was temporarily relieved as the Russian winter offensive gradually died away. The Red Army after nearly eight months of continuous forward movement had a last given the German Army respite. However, unbeknown to Army Group South, the Russians were preparing for a massive attack against the German centre, which was to carry them to the banks of the river Vistula in Poland. The German Army was soon to be vanquished forever from the Soviet Union.

During operations on the Eastern Front is a flak gun crew preparing for another fire mission. During the latter half of the war, as heavier and more lethal Soviet armour was brought to bear against the German Army, German forces clamoured to obtain more flak guns that could deal with the increasing enemy threat. By the second half of 1944 flak guns were being used against the steel tracks of the T-34 tank.

PaK crew out in the field during operations in the early winter of 1944. The gun is a PaK 7.5cm 97/38, which first saw its début on the Eastern Front in the summer of 1944. While the gun had limited effectiveness, it remained in service until the end of the war.

A 7.5cm leIG18 position in 1944. This weapon was one of the first post-World War One guns to be sued to the Wehrmacht and later the SS. The gun was light and robust and employed a shotgun breech action.

A flak gun sited on a flatbed railway wagon to protect the train from aerial attack. Apart from its unique anti-aircraft capability the flak gun could be used equally, or even better, against light armoured, soft skin vehicles, field fortifications and fortified buildings.

Wehrmacht troops crossing a rail line in 1944. The troop leader on the left raising his arm is armed with an MP38/40 machine pistol, while his comrades are equipped with the Kar98K bolt action rifle.

Here in a defensive position Wehrmacht troops use a shelter to sustain themselves on the front lines. The shelters which the Germans built were called *Halbgruppenunterstande* (half-group living bunkers). These were to become essential for the *Landser* if they were to survive the ceaseless artillery bombardments and terrible freezing weather conditions.

our photographs taken the moment a 15cm s.IG.33 is fired in anger against enemy positions. A typical infantry regiment controlled three infantry battalions, an infantry gun company with six 7.5cm IG18 and two 15cm s.IG33 guns, and an anti-tank company with twelve 3.7cm PaK35/36 guns. The 5cm s.IG33 infantry gun was regarded as the workhorse piece, operated by specially trained nfantrymen. Although the German soldier was capable of meeting the highest standards, fighting ourageously with self-sacrifice, he was fighting against massive numerical superiority and could only elay the enemy, not defeat it.

A column of troops in a variety of armoured vehicles during winter operations in 1944. In order to sustain their operational strength, troops were regularly compelled to move from one position to another. During daylight hours, moving columns of armour was often perilous, and as a result led to heavy casualties from enemy aerial attack.

Positioned out in a snowy field is an anti-aircraft gun with its crew. The gun's high velocity and flat trajectory made it a very accurate and effective in both an anti-aircraft and anti-tank role. These guns were lethal weapons to enemy aircraft.

A mortar crew putting together their 8cm sGrW 34 mortar for a fire mission during operations in 1944. It was very common for infantry, especially during intensive long periods of action, to fire their mortar from either trenches or dug-in positions where the mortar crew could also be protected from enemy fire.

Two photographs showing soldiers in a forward observation po surveying enemy positions through a pair of scissor binoculars. From this position the men could send details of enemy movements back to divisional headquarters.

In the snow, anti-tank gunners prepare their weapon for a fire mission against a Red Army target. The PaK gun provided both the Waffen-SS and Wehrmacht with not only effective fire support but also defensive staying power as troops found themselves confronted everywhere by increasing numbers of enemy tanks.

A whitewashed halftrack with a mounted 2cm flak gun complete with ammunition trailer during operations on the Eastern Front in the winter of 1944.

A 10.5cm heavy howitzer crew pose for the camera. Even during the last months of the war combat experience soon showed that artillery support was of decisive importance in both defensive and offensive roles. It was primarily the artillery regiments that were given the task of destroying enemy positions and fortified defences and conducting counter-battery fire prior to an armoured assault.

Out in the snow, a Wehrmacht mortar crew can be seen with the standard German mortar, the 8cm Granatwerfer 34 or Gr.W.34 mortar. The mortar's maximum range was 2.4 km when it fired the standard Wurfgranate 34 round which carried 550g of explosive. The round could be set to detonate on impact or in an airburst. It could also fire the Wurfgranate 40, a larger round with an increased explosive charge of almost 5kg. However this decreased the maximum range to 950m.

A photograph showing the moment a 10.5cm heavy howitzer is fired against an enemy target. The piece is a modified 10.5cm le FH 18/42. The 10.5cm was the standard light artillery piece deployed in the artillery divisions on the Eastern Front. However, in order to give the gun better punch on the battlefield the weapon was modified in 1942. The barrel was lengthened, a cage muzzlebrake was fitted, and the carriage was a lightened version of the le FH 18 design.

Positioned out in the snow is a 10.5cm heavy field howitzer. Even during the withdrawal in the second half of 1943, combat experience soon showed that artillery support was of decisive importance in both defensive and offensive roles.

An MG42 crew pause during operations on the Eastern Front in 1944. MG42 machine gun belts can be seen hung around their shoulders.

A mortar crew in action. A mortar crew usually consisted of at least three members. The gunner controlled the deflection and elevation of the weapon, the assistant gunner loaded the round at the command of the gunner, and the ammunition man prepared and handed over ammunition to the assistant gunner.

Well concealed in a field is a 7.5cm PaK40. The PaK40 had a spaced-armour shield which was held together by large bolts. These bolts also had drilled holes that allowed the crews to thread foliage through them.

MG34 machine gun crews take cover behind a mound during action in the summer of 1943. The MG34 was very effective in both defensive and offensive roles.

A photograph showing pioneers with their six-metre medium pneumatic boat. A number of heavy pieces of equipment could also be loaded onto these boats, which included the 8cm mortar, the 2cm anti-aircraft gun and the 7.5cm infantry gun.

A photograph taken the moment a 10.5cm gun crew fire their gun during a fire mission. One of the crew members plugs his ears as the weapon is in full recoil after it blasts its shell across a field.

A photograph taken the moment a 15cm heavy howitzer is fired in anger. This weapon remained the second most common artillery piece in SS service and served until the end of the war. `

Three Wehrmacht troops pose for the camera with local Russian women. It was not uncommon that Russian civilians were drafted in to help German troops dig defensive positions such as shelters and tank traps.

Chapter 3
Battle of Attrition

FROM RETREAT TO DEFEAT
PART I: WINTER 1944/45–MAY 1945

By May 1944 the Army Group had been ground down through a battle of attrition and as a consequence could no longer sustain itself cohesively on the battlefield. For months the German Army had fought desperately to maintain unity and hold its positions, at the cost of thousands of lives. It now not only lacked weapons and equipment but suffered serious shortages of manpower. The heavy drain of powerful Panzer units and other elite forces to the Western Front and north Ukraine had left the centre of the German Eastern Front very weak, without proper armour and aircraft support. In mid-June 1944 Army Group Centre had thirty-four infantry divisions, two Panzergrenadier divisions, two Luftwaffe field divisions, seven security divisions and just one Panzer division. To the rear were several Hungarian divisions, but these troops were badly under strength and unable to support the main German force for any appreciable length of time. In total the German Army had the equivalent of 52 divisions, with some 420,000 troops, and a further 400,000 in support. Although on paper this was considered to be a substantial force, the German infantry divisions during that summer were stretched beyond their limits. The front line which the German soldiers were supposed to defend was immense. Each division was supposed to defend a 12 to 16 mile front, but every mile was on average only protected by sixty frontline infantry, supported by two or three artillery pieces and a handful of assault guns.

To make matters worse, the quality of these soldiers had declined rapidly through the year, due to the enormous casualties. Since 1943 they were steadily replaced with troops of the *Volksdeutsche*, and ethnic Germans drafted from Eastern Europe. Although this bolstered the frontline German units, generally neither the *Volksdeutsche* nor the ethnic Germans were strong enough to withstand powerful Red Army assaults. With combat performance far reduced, even the strongest German infantry units were beginning to display low morale.

Defeat seemed imminent and yet the Germans were once again spared from total destruction as the Soviet offensive in the centre petered out. The temporary lull gave the German Army enough time to build a number of defensive positions. In the Belorussian sector, for instance, where the front had been relatively static for some months, the Germans feverishly constructed lines of trenches reinforced with machine gun and mortar pits. There were defensive belts heavily mined, most of them protected by extensive barbed wire barriers and some anti-tank guns.

In spite of the heavily fortified string of defensive lines, the fortifications were still inadequate. They were up against some 1,700,000 Red Army troops and support personnel – more than double the total German force – all preparing to launch a new massive offensive against Army Group Centre.

On the morning of 22 June 1944, three years to the day since the German Army had begun its campaign on the Eastern Front, the Russians finally unleashed their long-awaited offensive. The codename was 'Operation Bagration', and it opened up with a massive artillery bombardment intended to smash German defensive positions and annihilate Army Group Centre. The Russian 1st Baltic and 3rd Belorussian Fronts attacked northwest and southeast of the city of Vitebsk. The 3rd Panzer Army was taken completely by surprise. During the course of the day as the German defence lines began to crack under the mighty hammer blows of Russian artillery and attacking armour, the 3rd Panzer Army fought a desperate battle of attrition. The next day the Russians tore through the 3rd Panzer Army and closed its mighty jaws around the smouldering city of Vitebsk. On 24 June the 9th Army, still in a state of confusion from the massive Russian attack, was penetrated by the 1st Belorussian Front near the Beresina. Almost immediately the front begun to collapse under the pressure, leaving many units either encircled or totally annihilated. By the end of the fourth day Army Group Centre had committed all its reserves without stemming or even temporarily halting the Soviet drive. Already five German divisions were encircled and Vitebsk was almost lost. All over the front confusion swept through the German divisions. Other divisions that had not been severely mauled attempted to hold vital lines. The 3rd Panzer Army, for instance, tried desperately to cling to the Dvina and Ulla Rivers fifty miles west of Vitebsk, but could only hold out for a short time. As for the 9th Army, its troops were enduring some of the heaviest ground and aerial attacks that it had ever experienced.

Near Bobruisk the situation was critical. Some 40,000 troops were now trapped inside a pocket measuring about thirteen miles in diameter east of the city. A series of desperate breakouts were undertaken, but the Russian artillery and Air Force together turned it into a slaughter. Even the 12th Panzer Division, which had been hurried from Army Group North, could not help relieve the siege around the city. By 28 June the 9th Army was almost destroyed; 4th Army was in full retreat, and 3rd Panzer Army was penetrated in a number of places and barely able to maintain its forces cohesively.

Nevertheless, Hitler was adamant that his troops hold another line of defence. In less than a week's fighting the Germans had lost some 70,000 troops killed and captured. Even falling back to another defence line could not prevent the inevitable wholesale destruction of Army Group Centre. By early July most of the Army Group was trapped east of the city of Minsk by advancing Russian columns.

The bitter defensive fighting had cost Army Group Centre twenty-five divisions. The 4th Army had suffered terrible losses with some 130,000 lost out of its original strength of 165,000 men. The 3rd Panzer Army had lost ten divisions. The 9th Army was badly shattered along with remnants of the once-powerful 2nd Army. In total 28 divisions with more than 400,000 men had been captured. The destruction of Army Group Centre was the greatest single defeat of the German Army of the Second World War. It had suffered a defeat far greater than that of the 6th Army at Stalingrad. The successful conclusion of 'Operation Bagration' had effectively sealed the coffin of the German Army in the east. What was left of its mangled and exhausted forces limped westward into Poland to begin a reinforcement of the Vistula River line.

As for the Russian Army they were once again victorious. They had covered some 200 miles during the offensive without pause and were now deep in liberated territory.

A six metre inflatable boat has been pressed into service by assault troops. Two paddles either side was normally sufficient for the boats to be propelled through the water, even when carrying a full complement of infantry onboard with heavy weapons and equipment.

Two photographs showing the 8cm sGrW 34 mortar. One photograph shows the soldier looking through an optical range finder that has been attached to the gun tube. The other photograph shows a mortar trooper next to his weapon prior to a fire mission. It was very common for infantry, especially during intensive long periods of action, to fire their mortar from either trenches or dug-in positions where the mortar crew could also be protected from enemy fire.

Two photographs showing the lethal Nebelwerfer 41 in a field. The Nebelwerfer 41 was equipped with six barrels, each firing a 34 kg 150 mm Wurfgranate 41 (rocket shell 41) out to a range of approximately 6,800 metres. Along the German front the Nebelwerfer was used extensively and caused high losses in the Russian lines. This deadly weapon fired its shells from a six-tube mounted rocket launcher. When fired the projectiles screamed through the air, which terrified the enemy. These weapons served in independent army rocket launcher battalions, and in regiments and brigades.

A mortar crewman inside a dug-in 8cm sGrW 34 mortar position preparing to look through a pair of 6x30 Zeiss binoculars. Life in the line for these soldiers was a continuous grind, but any let-up in defence would ensure that the Red Army would push deeper into the German defences. German commanders in the field were well aware of the disasters befalling their comrades in the central and southern sectors of the front, and knew that their position on the Eastern Front was becoming more precarious with each passing day.

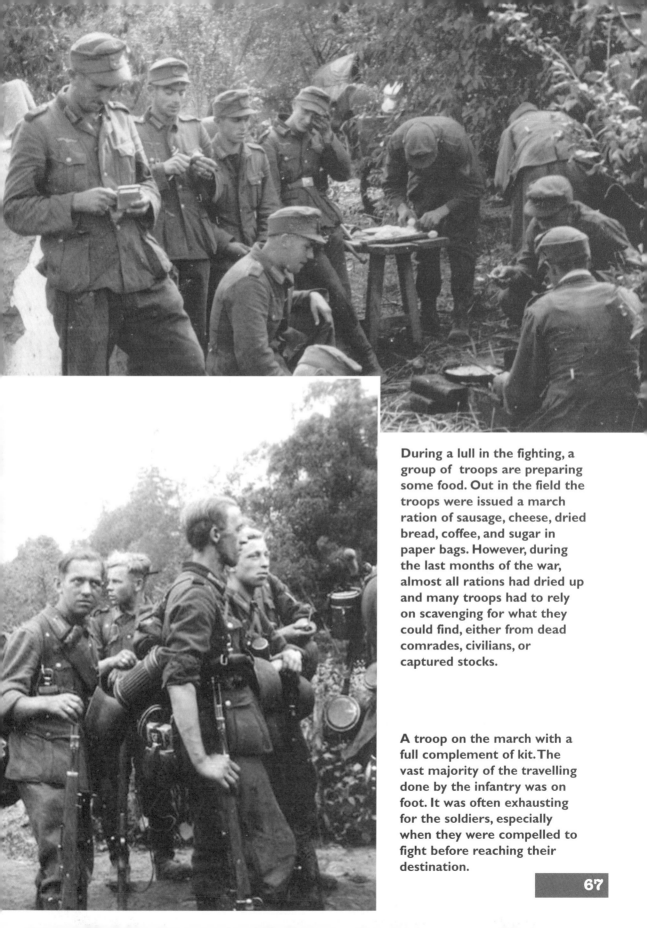

During a lull in the fighting, a group of troops are preparing some food. Out in the field the troops were issued a march ration of sausage, cheese, dried bread, coffee, and sugar in paper bags. However, during the last months of the war, almost all rations had dried up and many troops had to rely on scavenging for what they could find, either from dead comrades, civilians, or captured stocks.

A troop on the march with a full complement of kit. The vast majority of the travelling done by the infantry was on foot. It was often exhausting for the soldiers, especially when they were compelled to fight before reaching their destination.

Two shirtless soldiers clean their bolt action rifles during a lull in the fighting. On a number of sectors of the front the Wehrmacht managed to contain their Soviet foe and built strong fortified positions. While many of the positions were not

One of the most important forms of defensive action in any battle was communication from the front lines to the command post. Here in this photograph a radio man can be seen with his radio set communicating to one of the many field posts scattered in the rear.

A well concealed heavy MG42 machine gun crew. A typical strongpoint deployed along the German front comprised mainly of light and heavy MG34 and MG42 machine guns, anti-tank rifle company or battalion, a sapper platoon that was equipped with a host of various explosives, infantry guns, anti-tank artillery company which had a number of anti-tank guns, and occasionally a self-propelled gun.

A vehicle can be seen trying to negotiate a small roadway. Behind the vehicle, troops are seen digging trying to widen the road in order to allow more traffic to pass through unhindered.

In a fixed defensive position is a 2cm flak crew. The troops were now courageously battling from one receding front to another. Thousands of these flak guns were used in a desperate attempt to delay the Russian onslaught. However, like so much of the German arsenal employed in the east, they were too few or too dispersed to make any significant impact on the main Soviet operations, which were already capturing or encircling many of the key towns and cities.

One of the many dugout positions that were built along the Eastern Front. This is more than likely a forward observation post. Note the field telephone. Zeltbahn shelter quarters have been improvised to shelter the post from rain and wind. Note both dugouts have troops resting inside and their feet are protruding out.

A gunner can be seen with his 2cm Flakvierling 38 quadruple self-propelled flak gun. In November 1943 the Heer took over responsibility of the Luftwaffe field divisions. It quickly attempted to make drastic improvements in order to help prevent further massive losses and bolster their equipment and manpower so that they could support the army and Waffen-SS without disintegrating on the front lines.

One of the quickest methods of moving men and equipment from one part of the front to another was by rail. Here special flatbed rail cars are seen carrying vehicles and supplies. Note the MG34 machine gun on its tripod complete with barrel and machine gunner sitting on a chair next to his weapon. This gun was used for local defence against the ever increasing enemy aerial attacks.

A posed photograph showing two soldiers; one on the right is armed with the MP38/40 machine gun, and the other with the standard army issue Karbiner 98K bolt action rifle.

A very well concealed flak gunner with his flak gun out in the field. By 1944 many units were applying increasing amounts of foliage over their weapons in order to help minimise the incredible losses that were being sustained on the battlefield.

Many of the German army divisions, even by 1944, used mainly animal draught. Here in this photograph a long column of horses with soldiers can be seen in the rain. The bulk of the column is pulling supplies.

Two photographs showing troops during a march. The distances which the soldiers had to travel were immense. The fear of being constantly attacked by air caused many columns to move during the night.

A 2cm flak position in southern Russia. Although these light anti-aircraft guns were used extensively to deal with the threat of the Soviet Air Force, the recurring appearance of heavier enemy armour compelled many flak crews to divert their attention from the air and support their own infantry and armour on the ground in an anti-tank role.

An artillery observation post and a group of Wehrmacht personnel can be seen at a forward observation post. In the field a commanding officer can be seen looking through a pair of high powered 10x80 flak binoculars attached to a tripod. Behind them is a soldier looking through a 6x30 Sf.14Z Scherefernrohr or scissor binoculars. Each artillery or flak battery had an observation post among the frontline positions.

During a lull in the fighting the crew of a 10.5cm field howitzer can be seen sitting with their weapon. The 10.5cm field howitzer provided the division with a relatively effective mobile base of fire. It was primarily the artillery regiments that were given the task of destroying enemy positions and fortified defences and conducting counter-battery fire prior to an armoured assault.

Troops rest in a field during a lull in the fighting. Although the Germans were poorly matched in terms of equipment, the troops were often hardened veterans who had survived some of the most costly battles in the east, and they fought superbly to hold back the enemy.

German soldiers survey two knocked out T34 tanks.

A German soldier poses in front of a knocked out Soviet tank in the early winter of 1944.

A machine gunner armed with an MP38/40 machine gun. Next to him on its bipod is an MG34 machine gun.

A halftrack negotiates across a waterlogged field. A sudden downpour of rain could often turn roads and surrounding fields into boggy mires of mud and water, often making it virtually impossible for wheeled vehicles or animal draught to move through.

A motorcycle combination utilising animal draught to help it along a muddy road. Note how emaciated the horse appears. It is probable that the horse has been taken from a local Russian farmstead and used by the Army. The high use of animal draught in the German divisions, coupled with the massive losses of horses due to sickness, fatigue and being killed in battle, resulted in many thousands being taken from farms and the local population.

Here a Volkswagen Kubelwagen 82 has been transported from one side of a river to another, and its crew are preparing to move it up the embankment.

Chapter 4
Defending Poland

FROM RETREAT TO DEFEAT
PART II: WINTER 1943/44–AUTUMN 1944

By incredible efforts and courageous fighting the German Army managed to slow down the Russian offensive on the central sector of the Eastern Front. Throughout July Army Group Centre was withdrawing steadily through Poland. Its weary soldiers had been forced back towards Kaunas, the Neman River and Bialystok. The last of the German infantry units capable of retreating along the Warsaw highway over the Vistula at Siedlce was undertaken and assisted by the crack Waffen-SS division Totenkopf and the Luftwaffe's Hermann Göring Division. The whole German position in the east was now crumbling, and any hope of repairing it was made almost impossible by crippling shortages of troops. German infantry divisions continued desperately trying to fill the dwindling ranks. However, by the end of July the Red Army was already making good progress towards the Polish capital, Warsaw. On 7 August 1944 the Soviet offensive finally came to a halt east of Warsaw. Feldmarschall Model sent Hitler an optimistic report telling him that Army Group Centre had finally set up a continuous front from the south of Shaulyay to the right boundary on the River Vistula near Pulawy. The new front itself in Poland stretched some 420 miles and was manned by thirty-nine divisions and brigades. Although the force seemed impressive the German Army was actually weak; the divisions were under-strength, and were thinly-stretched. With these, the Germans were compelled to hold large areas along the Vistula River, which included Warsaw. What made matters worse was the fact that they faced a Russian force that was a third of the total Red Army. To the Germans, Warsaw possessed great strategic importance due to the vital traffic arteries running north-south and east-west, which crossed into the city. The Germans knew that if they wanted to keep control of the Eastern Front, they must hold onto the city at all costs.

As news reached Warsaw that the Russians were approaching, the Polish Home Army rose against the German forces in what became known as the Warsaw Uprising. In the north of the city the 4th and 19th Panzer Divisions, together with the Herman Göring Division, saw extensive action in trying to repulse the uprising. While the fighting raged inside the capital, north of the city Soviet troops had already made some impressive gains by pushing the 2nd Army towards the Narew River. Fortunately for the German troops the Red Army were too exhausted and the offensive ground to a halt.

But the lull in Poland was not mirrored elsewhere. In the north, Soviet forces were already in East Prussia threatening the German forces in that area by reaching the Baltic and cutting off Army Group North. In southern Poland the 1st Ukrainian Front captured Lemberg, while Romania fell to the 2nd and 3rd Ukrainian Fronts. Soviet forces had also penetrated Hungary, and its powerful armoured forces soon reached the capital, Budapest. On 20 August, the 2nd Ukrainian Front broke through powerful German defences, and the Red Army reached the Bulgarian border on 1 September. Within a week, Soviet troops arrived along the Yugoslav frontier. On 8 September, Bulgaria and Romania then declared war on Germany. It seemed that nothing but a series of defeats now plagued the German Army during the summer of 1944.

In a radical effort to stem the series of setbacks, General Heinz Guderian, Chief of the General staff, proposed that thirty divisions of Army Group North, which were redundant in Kurland, be shipped back to the Homeland so they could be re-supplied and re-strengthened to reinforce Army Group Centre in Poland. Hitler, however, emphatically refused Guderian's proposal.

As a consequence of Hitler's negative response, by October Army Group North was, as predicted, cut off, leaving 4th Army with only four weak corps to defend East Prussia against the full might of the Soviet forces. In Army Group Centre the 3rd Panzer Army and 4th Army were holding tenaciously to a weak salient in the north, while to the southwest, along the Narew River, the 2nd Army was still holding the river line. Army Group A had dug a string of defences from Modlin to Kaschau, with the 9th Army positioned either side of Warsaw along the Vistula. The 4th Panzer Army had dug in at Baranov and was holding positions against strong Russian attacks. The 17th Army had fortified its positions with a string of machine gun posts and mines between the Vistula and the Beskides, while the 1st Panzer Army was holding the area of Kaschau and Jaslo.

For the remaining weeks of 1944 the German Army defended Poland with everything it could muster. The bulk of the forces left to defend the frontlines were exhausted and undermanned. With reserves almost non-existent the dwindling ranks were bolstered by old men and low-grade troops. Struggling to find more manpower, convalescents and the medically unfit were also drafted into the ranks into what were known as 'stomach and ear' battalions because most men were hard of hearing or suffered from ulcers. Poland it seemed would be defended at all costs, despite the age and quality of the soldiers that manned the lines.

During an intensive fire action, an 8cm sGrW 34 mortar is loaded and fired in anger against an enemy target. Note how all the crew duck for cover to avoid the back blast as the projectile leaves the gun tube. Two of the ammunition handlers or loaders can be seen holding the tripod in order to keep it steady and accurate when firing. This mortar earned a deadly reputation on the Eastern Front and captured 34s were eagerly employed back against the Germans.

Wehrmacht anti-tank gunners rest in their defensive position in a field. Foliage has been applied to the piece and the gunners have also camouflaged their M35 helmets with foliage in order to try to conceal themselves. The PaK gun provided both the Army and the Waffen-SS with not only effective fire support but also defensive staying power as troops found themselves confronted everywhere by increasing numbers of enemy tanks.

Out in the field and a battery of camouflaged 15cm s.FH18 heavy field howitzers are being readied for action. The 15cm field howitzer was designed to attack targets deeper in the enemy rear. This included command posts, reserve units, assembly areas, and logistic facilities. Note the stacked pile of wicker ammunition cases.

An interesting photograph showing two stationary Soviet T-34 tanks in 1944 that have been captured and pressed into service by the Germans.

Two photographs showing modified 10.5cm le FH 18/42. Throughout the war the 10.5cm gun provided both the Heer and the Waffen-SS with a versatile, relatively mobile, base of fire. The 10.5cm was the standard light artillery piece deployed in the artillery divisions on the Eastern Front. However, in order to give the gun better punch on the battlefield the weapon was modified in 1942. The barrel was lengthened, a cage muzzle brake was fitted, and the carriage was a lightened version of the le FH 18 design.

The Germans had large quantities of captured weapons to either replace their depleted numbers or simply increase their firepower. Here in this photograph the Germans have pressed this Russian 76.2mm M1939 gun into service. The Germans designated this piece as a 7.62cm FK 297(r) or FK 39(r) field cannon.

A shirtless Infantryman stands beside a *Halbgruppenunterstande* shelter during operations in early 1944.

A mortar crew prepare their weapon for action. The Germans enjoyed considerable standardisation in mortar types with three basic weapons, though production shortfalls ensured that a range of foreign mortars served in both the Army and the Waffen-SS.

A light MG42 machine gun crew out in a field. The view from here would have offered an excellent opportunity for the gunner to detect enemy movement from some distance away.

An Sd.kfz.251 halftrack advances along a road. The MG34 machine gunner aims his weapon for local fire support. During the war the Sd.Kfz.251 had become not just a halftrack intended to transport infantry to the edge of the battlefield, but also a fully-fledged fighting vehicle.

Troops with the standard 15cm Nebelwerfer 41. Because it was dangerous for the crew to remain close to the launcher while the piece was being fired, it was fired remotely using an electrical detonator attached to a cable, which ran to the piece.

The crew of a 10.5cm heavy field howitzer is in a field during a lull in the fighting and waiting for the order to resume firing again. Ammunition is stacked in special crates. Note the gun's aiming stake is being temporarily used as tent pole.

A photograph taken the moment a Wespe fires a projectile from its recoiled 10.5cm le.FH 18/2 L/28 gun. The crew inside the vehicle are protected by a light armoured superstructure mounted on the chassis of a Pz.Kpfw.II. The vehicles served in armoured artillery battalions but were lightly armoured, and as result many of them were lost in battle.

A mortar crew pose for the camera during a lull in the fighting. A mortar crew usually consisted of at least three members. A mortar crew usually consisted of at least three members. The gunner controlled the deflection and elevation of the weapon; the assistant gunner loaded the round at the command of the gunner; and the ammunition man prepared and handed over ammunition to the assistant gunner.

One of the most impressive mortars used by the Germans on the Eastern Front was the 12cm Granatwerfer 378(r), pictured in these two photographs. The weapon consisted of a circular base plate, the tube and the supporting bipod, and it weighed 285kg. Because of its weight, a two wheeled axle was utilised, enabling the mortar to be towed into action. The axle could then be quickly removed before firing. The weapon fired the Wurfgranate 42 round, which carried 3.1 kg of explosive.

A group of German troops including rifleman and two **MG34** machine gunners can be seen in their full battle dress with their commander. Zeltbahn waterproof quarters are being worn over their standard issue uniform to afford protection against the damp and wet of the forest. Shoved in their black leather infantryman belts are the **Stg24** stick grenade. Their M35 steel

One method of travel for infantry was by bicycle. Here a squad of bicycle infantrymen have dismounted under the protection of a tree. Note the troop leader armed with a 9mm MP38/40 machine-pistol. The MP38/40 machine pistol was commonly known as the Schmeisser.

A group of Sd.Kfz. 251/17 halftracks. These modified halftracks were known as the *Schützenpanzerwagen* (2 cm). They were anti-aircraft vehicles armed with a 2 cm KwK38 on a pedestal mounting with a small armoured turret to protect the gunner. Later in the war, these vehicles were issued as a platoon commander's vehicle to replace the Sd.Kfz. 251/10.

A Jagdpanzer IV is seen going through a town. The superstructure had sloping surfaces and a periscope for crew vision atop a Pz.Kpfw.IV chassis. The tank destroyer was armed with 7.5cm PaK39 supported by two front mounted machine guns.

An interesting photograph showing a flak gun mounted on the rear of a truck during summer operations. The vehicle and piece are both well concealed from enemy aerial attack or ground surveillance.

Three different photographs in a forward observation post showing a mounted 6x30 Sf.14Z Scherenfernrohr (scissor binoculars). These are more than likely artillery observation posts searching for enemy targets.

Here a PaK crew manhandles a Pak 35/36 across rough terrain to a new position. This weapon was the first anti-tank gun mass produced and saw service in both the Heer and the Waffen-SS. It was also used extensively on the Eastern Front, and went on to be used until the end of the war. An anti-tank company comprised twelve 3.7cm PaK35/36 guns.

German foot soldiers on the move during operations in southern Russia. Black smoke and dust is visible indicating that these men are under battlefield conditions.

A quadruple flak gun, served by eight men, was a deadly piece of weaponry. These lethal guns were much respected by low-flying Russian airmen and were also particularly devastating against light vehicles, as well as troops caught out in the open.

Three photographs showing a decoration
ceremony in 1944.

Commanding officers conferring, sitting at the side of a building. Note the map case lying just forward of the small entrenchment that has been dug around the building.

Rocket artillery comprised of several types of pieces including the standard 15cm Nebelwerfer 41. Here troops roll this Nebelwerfer out of a wooded area to position it for a fire action. The carriage that the piece is mounted on derives from that of a 3.7cm PaK35/36.

This PaK crew have expertly camouflaged their PaK 3.7cm PaK35/36. They have very effectively disguised the outline of their piece, while leaving an excellent field of fire to their front.

A mortar crew can be seen on the march through a wooded area. A mortar crew usually comprised of three soldiers: the gunner, the assistant gunner, and an ammunition handler.

Soldiers pose for the camera wearing animal skin coats to keep them warm. These animal skin coats varied greatly in size and quality, and they were primarily designed to be worn in extreme cold climates. They were normally worn by officers, as in this photograph, but soldiers were also seen wearing them, especially on guard duties.

A group of soldiers pose for the camera after being decorated with the Iron Cross.

Soldiers struggle to move supplies being pulled by animal draught. With the loss of many vehicles on the front the dependence on horse power for transporting weapons and supplies became ever greater.

Here shirtless 7.5cm l.IG18 gunners are seen with their piece during summer operations in 1944. This particular weapon was used in direct infantry support. The gun was very versatile in combat and the crew often aggressively positioned it, which usually meant the piece was frequently exposed on the battlefield.

Here soldiers negotiate a river crossing using a fallen tree. The soldier leading the crossing is armed with the StG 44 or Sturmgewehr 44 (assault rifle), which was the first modern assault rifle. It was also known as the MP 43 or MP 44 (Maschinenpistole 43/44). The StG 44 played a very successful role in combat, particularly on the Eastern Front, offering a greatly increased volume of fire compared to standard infantry rifles and greater range than sub-machine guns.

Soldiers relax during a pause in the fighting and listen to a comrade playing an accordion.

During a training exercise these PaK gunners are seen with the famous PaK35/36 anti-tank gun. These guns by 1944 were outdated and inadequate against Russian armour, but crews still trained with them, and they were used on the Eastern Front in combat until the end of the war.

A soldier poses for the camera wearing his M38 field cap and holding his M35 steel helmet.

Riflemen advance through a town. All of the men are armed with the standard issue Karbine 98K bolt action rifle, and one of them can be seen holding a box of ammunition.

During heavy fighting riflemen armed with the bolt action rifle can be seen in a defensive position. Note the shelter: the *Halbgruppenunterstande* (group and half-group living shelter).

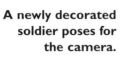

A newly decorated soldier poses for the camera.

Soldiers under battlefield conditions are seen taking cover wearing their reversible snow suits. Note the captured Soviet PPsh sub-machine gun laying on an ammunition box next to a stick grenade. In the field, the PPSh was a durable, low-maintenance weapon that could fire 900 rounds/min. Some six million of these weapons had been produced by the end of the war, and the Soviets would often equip whole regiments and even entire divisions with the weapon. The gun had proven such an effective weapon on the battlefield that both the German Army and the Waffen-SS used captured stocks extensively throughout the fighting on the Eastern Front.

A squad leader can be seen dressed in full battlefield dress with equipment. He is armed with the MP38/40 machine pistol, 6x30 binoculars, map case and ammunition pouches. He also wears a whitewashed M35 steel helmet.

Troops during winter operations are seen armed with an MG34 machine gun, and the MP38/40. They all wear the new reversible winter uniform. The garment was designed large enough to be worn over the German army field service uniform including the basic field equipment. However, the majority of soldiers preferred wearing their equipment over the winter jacket. Although the winter reversible was a popular item of clothing it soon became dirty from constant wear and defeated the objective of the white camouflage.

Men, vehicles and PaK guns can be seen on a road somewhere on the Eastern Front. Despite the adverse situation in which the German Army was placed, soldiers continued to fight in a bitter and frantic struggle to prevent the Red Army from reaching the frontiers of the Reich. Deluged by an armada of tanks, mass infantry assaults, and the constant hammer blows of Russian artillery, the German Army along with its fanatical SS counterparts fought a series of vicious battles through the Baltic States and Byelorussia, before building up new defences along the Vistula in Poland.

Armed with the MP38/40 machine pistol this squad leader wears another form of winter camouflage which was rarely seen in later war periods – the snow overall. It was long and covered the entire service uniform and was designed to reach the wearer's ankles. It was shapeless, had buttons right down the front, a deep collar, an attached hood and long sleeves. The black infantryman's leather belt and personal equipment was often worn attached around the outside the garment in order to allow better access to it.

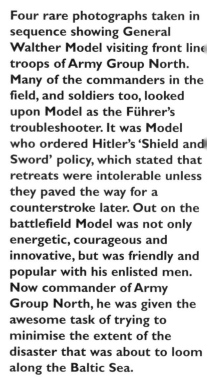

Four rare photographs taken in sequence showing General Walther Model visiting front line troops of Army Group North. Many of the commanders in the field, and soldiers too, looked upon Model as the Führer's troubleshooter. It was Model who ordered Hitler's 'Shield and Sword' policy, which stated that retreats were intolerable unless they paved the way for a counterstroke later. Out on the battlefield Model was not only energetic, courageous and innovative, but was friendly and popular with his enlisted men. Now commander of Army Group North, he was given the awesome task of trying to minimise the extent of the disaster that was about to loom along the Baltic Sea.

Chapter 5
Army in Retreat

FROM RETREAT TO DEFEAT
PART III: WINTER 1944/45–MAY 1945

The year 1944 ended with the German Army still fighting on foreign soil trying desperately to gain the initiative and throw the Red Army back from its remorseless drive on the German frontier. But despite the skill and determination shown by the German soldiers in late 1944, most of them were aware that 1945 would be fateful – the year of decision.

In January 1945 along the Vistula Front hope dawned among some of the more fanatical commanders of the German Army. The strongest of the forces deployed along the Vistula against the Russians were in Army Group Centre. Its battle line ran more than 350 miles. However, each division that was placed on the front lines was perilously under strength and would not be able to contain a Russian attack for any appreciable length of time. On 13 January 1945 the Soviet offensive opened up and soldiers and Panzer crews from the 4th Panzer Army bore the brunt of the attack on the Vistula. Almost immediately the army was engulfed in a storm of fire. Across the snow-covered terrain Red Army troops and massive numbers of armoured vehicles flooded the battlefield. By the end of the first day the battle had ripped open a breach more than twenty miles wide in the Vistula Front. The 4th Panzer Army was virtually annihilated. Small groups of German soldiers tried frantically to fight their way westwards through the flood of Red infantry and tanks.

As the whole German military campaign in the east began collapsing it was proposed that all German forces located between the Oder and Vistula rivers be amalgamated into a new army group named 'Army Group Vistula'. SS Reichsführer Heinrich Himmler was to command the new army group. German soldiers together with elite formations of the Waffen-SS were supposed to prevent the Soviets from breaking through. However, the once mighty German Army was now suffering from an unmistakable lack of provisions. By January 1945, the problems had become so critical that even children and old men were being thrown into what was now being called the last bastion of defence for the Reich. In Army Group Vistula the German Army could no longer function properly.

There was no contact between units on the battlefield, battalions were out of touch with their companies, and regiments had no link with their divisions. Successive blows by the Red Army began to tear apart Himmler's Army Group and send scattered German formations reeling back westward towards the Oder or north-westwards into Pomerania. As the whole front began withdrawing both the 9th Army and 2nd Army's right wings lost contact with each other. In a drastic measure to restore the disintegrating situation General Weiss, commanding the 2nd Army, tried to stabilise the front on the Vistula between the town of Thorn and Graudenz. But still Soviet forces were overwhelming many German positions and pushing back Hitler's exhausted forces.

Despite the best efforts of the German Army to bolster its dwindling ranks on the Eastern Front, nothing could now mask the fact that they were dwarfed by the superiority of the Red Army. It was estimated that the Russians had some six million men along a front which stretched from the Adriatic to the Baltic. To the German soldiers facing the Russians, the outcome was almost certain death. They were well aware that what they had done in Russia and the occupied territories had caused the Red Army to exact a terrible revenge.

As the Nazi empire was sheared off piece by piece, Dr Josef Goebbels, the Reich's propaganda chief, begun to switch from terror-mongering to reassuring the population that victory was just around the corner. However, in an atmosphere of near panic, stirred up by refugees and their stories of Russian atrocities, there was little to console them. Many stories had already reached the German front lines as to how the Red Army had raped and murdered women. The widespread panic among the civilians was causing the German command many problems, especially with supply and troop movements. In some areas the roads had become so congested with civilians and soldiers that many miles were brought to a complete standstill.

Out on the battlefield, the realisation among troops that they might lose the war was seldom admitted openly; but most of the soldiers already knew that the end would come soon. Troops were not convinced by their commanders' encouragements especially when they were lying in their trenches subjected to hours of bombardment by guns that never seemed to lack shells. Poorly armed and undermanned, infantry and Panzer divisions were exhausted shadows of their former selves.

The last great offensives that brought the Russians their final victory in Eastern Europe began during the third week of January 1945. Marshal Konev's 1st Ukrainian Front surged into Silesia after the capture of Radom and Krakow. On the night of 27 January, the German divisions of the 17th Army pulled out of the region towards the Oder River. The principal objective of the Red Army during late January 1945 was for an all-out assault along the Baltic to crush the remaining under-strength German units that had formed Army Group North. It was these heavy, sustained attacks that eventually restricted the German-held territory in the north-east to a few small pockets of land surrounding three ports: Libau in Kurland, Pillau in East Prussia and Danzig at the mouth of River Vistula. It was here along the Baltic that the German defenders attempted to stall the massive Russian onslaught with the few weapons and men they had at their disposal. Every German soldier defending the area was aware of the significance if it were captured. Not only would the coastal garrisons be cut off and eventually destroyed, but also masses of civilian refugees would be prevented from escaping from the ports by sea. Terrified civilians eager to board the next ships to the homeland queued night and day until the next vessel came in. They were so desperate to leave that they stood out in the open, enduring constant bombing and strafing by low-flying Russian aircraft, whose presence was now unchallenged in the sky.

For the next several weeks thousands of civilians risked their lives in order to escape from the clutches of the Red Army. Even to the end of March 1945, as Soviet troops fought their way into the outskirts of Gdynia, the German Navy continued rescuing many refugees before the Russians could get to them. German soldiers too, even remnants of elite Waffen-SS units, found themselves faced with a similar experience. Thousands of dishevelled troops streamed towards the coast, mingling with countless numbers of terrified women and children. Just along the coast in Danzig, the Russians stormed the ancient Teutonic city, smashing into the rear of fleeing German troops who were making their way desperately along the Vistula estuary. To the German soldiers that saw Danzig fall, it marked a complete disaster along the Baltic. Russian soldiers, however, saw Danzig as a way of exterminating Teutonic culture, which had long since been despised. All over the city, they blew up old buildings, set alight churches and randomly executed groups of soldiers that had not raised the white flag of surrender, but had fought on until they ran out of ammunition.

Elsewhere along the Baltic coast isolated areas of German resistance continued to fight on, but still they had no prospect of holding back the Russians. Hitler made it quite clear that Army Group Kurland was not to be evacuated. To the Führer, Kurland was the last bastion of defence in the east and every soldier, he said, was to 'stand and fight' and wage an unprecedented battle of attrition. In fact, what Hitler had done in a single sentence was to condemn to death some 8,000 officers and more than 181,000 soldiers and Luftwaffe personnel. Those soldiers who managed to escape the destruction of Army Group Kurland retreated back towards the River Oder or returned by ship to Germany.

On other parts of the Eastern Front fighting was merciless, with both sides imposing harsh measures on their men to stand where they were and fight to the death. Since September 1944, Hitler had appreciated the importance of holding the city of Breslau from the approaching Red Army and declared it a fortress. As with other towns and villages lining the approaches to the Homeland, Breslau's infantry formations consisted mainly of old men and young boys who were poorly-equipped and hastily trained for combat. Four months later in January 1945, the city was still poised for the arrival of the Russians. By February, the sound of approaching Russian guns brought the city to panic stations. It was the 269th Infantry Division, withdrawing in the face of the massive Soviet advance, that was given the objective of forming the main defence of Breslau.

To test the defenders of Breslau, the Red Army launched a series of probing attacks into the city. Four Soviet divisions then carried out a furious assault that penetrated Breslau's defences. Volkssturm, Hitlerjugend, Waffen-SS and various formations from the 269th Infantry Division put up a staunch defence with every available weapon they could muster. As the battle raged, both German soldiers and civilians were cut to pieces by Russian fire. The Red Army drive was so powerful and swift that by 14 February the city was cut off and isolated, miles behind the Russian front.

During these vicious battles, which continued into May 1945, after Berlin had fallen, there were many acts of courageous fighting. Cheering and yelling, old men and boys of the Volkssturm and Hitlerjugend advanced across open terrain into a barrage of machine gun and mortar fire. By the first week of March, Russian infantry had driven back the defenders into the inner city and were pulverising it street by street. Lightly-clad Volkssturm and Hitlerjugend were still resisting, forced to fight in the sewers beneath the ravaged city. Almost 60,000 Russian soldiers were killed or wounded trying to capture the city, with some 29,000 German military and civilian casualties. When Breslau finally capitulated, the Red Army was bitter and vented its anger against the civilians.

As the massive Russian forces pushed ever westward, the German Army, along with the Waffen-SS, Luftwaffe, Volkssturm and Hitlerjugend formations, withdrew under increasing pressure nearer and nearer to the Homeland. With every defeat and withdrawal came ever-increasing pressure on the commanders to exert harsher discipline on their weary men. The thought of fighting on German soil for the first time resulted in mixed feelings among the men. Although the defence of the Reich automatically stirred emotional feelings to fight for their land, many soldiers were quite openly aware that morale was being completely destroyed. They had all received a message from the Führer telling them to fight to the death, and they no longer had the manpower resources or strength to wage a bloody war of attrition. More young conscripts began showing signs that they did not want to die for a lost cause.

Conditions on the Eastern Front were miserable not only for the newest recruit, but also the battle-hardened veteran who had survived many months of bitter conflict against the Red Army. The cold harsh weather during February and March prevented the soldiers digging trenches more than a few feet deep. But the main problems that confronted the German Army during this period of the war were shortages of ammunition, fuel and vehicles. Some vehicles in the divisions could only be used in an emergency and troops were strictly prohibited from using them without permission from the commanding officer. The daily ration on average per division was for two shells per gun. Thousands of under-nourished civilians, mostly women and slave labourers, were marched out to expend all their available energy to dig lines of anti-tank ditches. For the benefit of the newsreel camera, which was intended somehow to help bolster the morale of the troops, Hitler made a secret visit on 13 March 1945 to the Oder Front. In fact, Hitler did not meet one ordinary soldier at the front and was surrounded by well-armed SS guards. During his brief war conference on the terrible situation faced by his Army, he gave a formal speech on the necessity of holding the positions. He told General Busse, commander of the

9th Army, to use all available weapons and equipment at his disposal to hold back the Russians.

However, nothing could stop the Red Army's drive. Out on the Vistula Front, German troops were now barely holding their wavering positions that ran some 175 miles from the Baltic coast to the juncture of the Oder and Neisse in Silesia. Most of the front was now held on the western bank of the Oder. In the north the ancient city of Stettin, and in the south the town of Küstrin, were both vital holding points against the main Russian objective of the war – Berlin.

By late March, the situation in Army Group Vistula had become much worse. Not only were supplies dwindling, but rations too were becoming so low that some soldiers were beginning to starve. In the ranks rations were more abundant: most days each soldier received an Army loaf and some stew or soup, which was often cold and not very appetising. But the main problem was the lack of clean drinking water. As a result of this, many of the soldiers suffered from dysentery.

The bulk of the Vistula front was manned by inexperienced training units. Some soldiers were so young that in their rations they were handed sweets instead of tobacco. More experienced soldiers observed that the Soviets were playing with them like 'cat and mouse'. Sitting in their trenches, cowering under the constant Soviet shelling, almost all of the men seemed fixated on one thing: 'the order to hurry up and retreat.'

Despite all its weaknesses on the Vistula Front, the German Army could still be a formidable opponent. Both young and old alike fought together to hold some kind of line in the face of the massive Russian onslaught.

In the last months of the war on the Eastern Front, German infantry divisions tried their best to form some kind of defensive line along an increasingly shrinking front. Exhausted and demoralised skeletal units that had been fighting for survival in previous weeks were now fully aware of the impending defeat in the east. Yet the German General Staff was still determined to fight at all costs, even if it meant throwing together unfit or badly depleted regiments and battalions.

In late March 1945, east of Berlin, German infantry and Panzer troops were compelled to hold the front against superior Soviet artillery and aviation. The German soldier had neither the manpower nor the weapons to hold the Russian onslaught, in spite of determined resistance along some sectors of the Front.

The Eastern Front, over which the German soldier had marched victoriously into heartlands of the Soviet Union in the summer of 1941, was now no more than 100 miles from the Reich capital. Between Berlin and the River Oder was a motley assortment of German soldiers, Waffen-SS, Volkssturm, Hitlerjugend and Luftwaffe troops preparing for the final onslaught of the Russian Army. When the final attack began on the River Oder on 16 April 1945 the German soldier was overwhelmed within days, and was slowly beaten back to the gates of Berlin. It was here that the German soldier fought out the last days of the war in the east until he was either captured or destroyed.

Panzergrenadiers dressed in winter white smocks are seen along a road full of advancing German armour. On 12 January 1945, the Eastern Front erupted with a massive advance, as Konev's offensive began, with the 1st Ukrainian Front making deep wide sweeping penetrations against hard-pressed German formations. The Russian offensive was delivered with a weight and fury never before experienced on the Eastern Front. On the first day of the offensive the 4th Panzer Army took the full brunt of an artillery barrage followed by an armoured attack by the 1st Byelorussian Front. It had overwhelming numerical superiority over the Germans, with 7 to 1 in armour alone.

Panzergreandiers hitching a lift on board what appears to be an **Pz.Kpfw.IV Ausf.G**. Sometimes the quickest method of moving from one battle area to another was on board a tank.

Two grenadiers dressed in white camouflage smocks have taken up a position in the snow. The soldier looking through his 6x30 binoculars is armed with the **Stg44 Sturmgewehr 44** (assault rifle), while his comrade can be seen aiming his **MG34** machine gun on a sustained fire mount.

Withdrawing from the front, grenadiers and vehicles can be seen moving along a road in the snow. While these soldiers had determinedly held out for a considerable length of time, supported by Panzers and anti-tank guns, they were soon overwhelmed by Russian superiority and to prevent complete annihilation were forced to fall back.

Here a soldier is fixing a broken part of a horse-drawn cart in the snow. By this stage of the war most of the supply vehicles were either destroyed in combat, broken from continuous use, or simply abandoned. Maintaining them was time consuming, but often vital to keep the front supplied.

Here mountain troops are seen with an MG42 on a sustained fire mount. The troops are wearing winter reversibles grey-side out.

A loader loads the Wurfgranate 42 round into the 12cm Granatwerfer 378(r) mortar. This powerful mortar could cause extensive damage to an enemy position, but was often not very accurate.

Artillerymen plug their ears in preparation for the firing of a 15cm field howitzer in early 1945 in the Baltic theatre. During the Battle of the Baltic the Germans and their Allies suffered from a serious lack of provisions. Units were thrown into battle wholesale, their commanders hoping that it would stem the enemy's drive through the Baltic states. To Hitler the Baltic states were the last bastion of defence on the northern front. Every soldier, he said, was to continue to 'stand and fight' and wage an unprecedented battle of attrition.

Troops withdraw through a town. Note the grenadier, armed with the deadly Panzerfaust. During the last year of the war the Panzerfaust was used extensively to combat Russian armour. It was a handheld rocket-propelled grenade.

A PaK crew pose for the camera. Anti-tank guns became one of the main pieces of weaponry the Germans used to defend their positions from the advancing Soviets. Along many parts of the front they proved very successful, but only at temporarily stemming the enemy drive.

A posed photograph showing grenadiers in front of a building wearing their Zeltbahn shelter quarters to keep them dry. Their kit is being worn over the garment so it can be accessed quickly.

One of the many Luftwaffe field units that were attached to the Heer during the latter part of the war. Here the troops wade through marshy land, probably in the Baltic region in 1945.

Grenadiers cross a stream on a makeshift bridge in early 1945 while withdrawing towards the Reich. By early February 1945 German forces in the east had been driven back to the River Oder, the last line of defence before Berlin. Only three weeks earlier, the Eastern Front was still deep in Poland. Now Upper Silesia was lost; in East Prussia German forces were smashed to pieces; West Prussia and Pomerania were being defended by depleted troops thrown together, and the defence of the Oder was now being entrusted to exhausted armies that had been fighting defensive actions for months in Poland along the Vistula. These forces were supposed to hold the Oder front and fight to the death.

Troops keep cover from heavy Russian fire along an embankment. Heavy rain has caused the position to become waterlogged and probably very uncomfortable for the soldiers forced to take up position here.

Grenadiers aid an injured comrade. The soldier is armed with the Sturmgewehr 44. The first batches of these guns were shipped to troops on the Eastern Front in 1944. By the end of the war, a total of 425,977 StG 44 of all variants were produced.

A typical road in the east has been churned up by continuous traffic. Here supply vehicles are approaching a river crossing.

Two grenadiers walk along a road. Behind the troop leader armed with an MP38/40 is a soldier armed with the lethal *Panzerschreck* or tank shocker. The popular name given by the troops for this weapon was the *Raketenpanzerbüchse* or rocket tank rifle, abbreviated to RPzB. It was an 8.8cm reusable anti-tank rocket launcher developed during the latter half of the war. Another popular nickname for it was the *Ofenrohr* or stove pipe.

A gunner with his mounted 3.7cm FlaK gun on a fixed camouflaged platform.

In a defensive position this MG34 machine gunner glares at the camera. The machine gun is fixed on a sustained fire mount and is well concealed.

A soviet tank being ferried across a river somewhere in the Baltic region in 1945.

An **MG42** machine gunner expertly concealed in undergrowth. His camouflaged steel helmet and splinter uniform blends well with the local surroundings.

Two photographs showing the *Panzerfaust* anti-tank projector. The Panzerfaust consisted of a small, disposable preloaded launch tube firing a high explosive anti-tank warhead, operated by a single soldier. The Panzerfaust remained in service in various versions until the end of the war. The weapon often had warnings written in large red letters on the upper rear end of the tube, warning the user of the back blast. After firing, the tube was discarded, making the Panzerfaust the first disposable anti-tank weapon.

A Flak crew are manhandling an 8.8cm Flak gun. With Soviet aircraft ruling the skies in the east many German divisions had increased their anti-aircraft battalions, with each of them containing two or even three heavy batteries. This photograph shows an 8.8cm flak gun complete with *Schützchild* (splinter shield). In some sectors of the front, some units barely had enough Panzers to oppose the Russian armour and called upon flak battalions to halt the Red Army's attacks. During this later period many flak guns came to be assigned dual purposes, which involved adding an anti-tank role to their operational duties. Note the kill rings on the barrel of this 8.8cm Flak gun.

Supplies of fuel are being loaded onto a vehicle to be taken to front line vehicles for refuelling. One of the major problems for vehicles on the Eastern Front by 1945 was the lack of fuel.

A soldier poses for the camera. In the last remaining weeks of the war there was almost no respite on the front line and the dwindling numbers of soldiers to man the already over-extended front was causing unprecedented problems.

In Army Group North horse drawn transport tows a 7.5cm I.IG18 across a frozen plain. During the Russian offensive in January and February 1945 troops of Army Group North found it next to impossible to contain the Soviet onslaught. Troops of the German 18th Army were beginning to disintegrate. Already it had incurred 40,000 casualties trying to contain the Soviets. Fighting in the mud and freezing water, the men were totally exhausted. Hitler on the other hand still prohibited all voluntary withdrawals and reserved all decisions to withdraw for himself. In a leadership conference held by the Führer the commanders were told to infuse determination in their men and to strengthen faith in ultimate victory. But in spite of Hitler's attempts to generate the will to fight, the German Army were unable to stem the rout of the advancing Russian forces.

Wearing their splinter camouflage smocks this Wurfgranate 42 heavy mortar crew have prepared their weapon for action. The tube length was 186.5cm and the complete weapon weighed 285kg.

In Army Group North grenadiers can be seen advancing through heavy foliage. One of the soldiers is armed with the Sturmgewehr 44 assault rifle.

A machine gunner advances along a road passing a burning building. Although a machine gun troop was normally a three man squad, due to the high casualty rates suffered on the Eastern Front by 1945, they were commonly reduced to just two, but still highly effective.

At a defensive position, commanding officers can be seen conferring in front of their shelter or *Halbgruppenunterstande* (group and half-group living bunkers).

gunners in a defensive position. This weapon is being used in an anti-tank role. Along
German front, divisions comprised of handfuls of anti-tank and artillery guns which
strung out along the front lines and were almost totally unprotected. A report noted
each division had to hold a frontage of approximately twenty miles. For every one
of front some remaining regiments had one artillery piece, one heavy machine gun,
light machine guns and about 150 men. On every two and a half miles of front they
in addition, one anti-tank gun.

Troops pose for the camera during the last weeks of the war. Conditions on the Eastern Front were miserable not only for the newest recruits, but also for battle-hardened soldiers who had survived many months of bitter conflict against the Red Army.

APPENDIX I

Hitler's 'Fortified Area' Order March 1944

The Führer
High Command of the Army
Führer Order No.11

Führer Headquarters
8th March 1944

(Commandants of Fortified Areas and Battle Commandants) In view of various incidents, I issue the following orders:

1. A distinction will be made between 'Fortified Areas', each under a 'Fortified Area Commandant', and 'Local Strong points', each under a 'Battle Commandant'. The 'Fortified Areas' will fulfil the functions of fortresses in former historical times. They will ensure that the enemy does not occupy these areas of decisive operational importance. They will allow themselves to be surrounded, thereby holding down the largest possible number of enemy forces, and establishing conditions for successful counter-attacks. Local strong points deep in the battle area, which will be tenaciously defended in the event of enemy penetrations. By being included in the main line of battle they will act as a reserve of defence and, should the enemy break through, as hinges and corner stones for the front, forming positions from which counter-attacks can be launched.

2. Each 'Fortified Area Commandant' should be a specially selected, hardened soldier, preferably of General's rank. The Army Group concerned will appoint him. Fortified Area commandants will be instructed to personally be responsible to the Commander-in-Chief of the Army Group. Fortified Area Commandants will pledge their honour as soldiers to carry out their duties to the last. Only the Commander-in-Chief of an Army Group in person may, with my approval, relieve the Fortified Area commandant duties, and perhaps order the surrender of the fortified area. Fortified Area Commandants are subordinate to the Commander of the Army Group, or Army, in whose sector the fortified area is situated. Further delegation of command to General officers commanding formations will not take place. Apart from the garrison and its security forces, all persons within a fortified area, or who have been collected there, are under the orders of the commandant, irrespective of whether they are soldiers or civilians, and without regard to their rank or

appointment. The Fortified Area Commandant has the military rights and disciplinary powers of a commanding General. In the performance of duties he will have at his disposal mobile courts-martial and civilian courts. The Army Group concerned will appoint the staff of Fortified Area Commandants. The Chiefs of staff will be appointed by High Command of the Army, in accordance with suggestions made by the Army Group.

3. The Garrison of a fortified area comprises: the security garrison, and the general garrison. The security garrison must be inside the fortified area at all times. Its strength will be laid down by Commander-in-Chief Army Group, and will be determined by the by the size of the area and the tasks to be fulfilled (preparation and completion of defences, holding the fortified area against raids or local attacks by the enemy). The general garrison must be made available to the Commandant of the fortified area in sufficient time for the men to have taken up defensive positions and be installed when a full-scale enemy threatens. It strength will be laid down by the Commander-in-Chief Army Group, in accordance with the size of the fortified area and the task which is to be performed (total defence of the fortified area).

Signed: ADOLF HITLER

APPENDIX II

Grenadier-Regiment 1944

Regiments-Stab	
Nachrichtenzug	
Pioniezug	6 x light MG34/42
Reiter-Oder Radfahrerzug	3 x light MG34/42
Grenadier-Bataillon (x2)	
Bataillons-Stab	
Schutzen-Kompanie (x3)	16 x light MG, 2 x 8cm mortar
Maschinengewehr-Kompanie	3 x light MG, 12 x heavy MG, 4 x 8cm mortar

Leichte Infanterie Kolonne
Infanteriegeschutz-Kompanie
5 x light MG, 6 x 7.5cm inf gun
2 x 15cm inf gun
Panzerjäger-Kompanie 13 x light MG, 12 x 7.5cm AT gun
Regiments Tross

Volksgrenadier-Regiment 1944/45

Volksgrenadier-Regiment 1944/45	
Regiments-Stab	
Stabs-Kompanie	10 x light MG34/42
Grenadier-Bataillon (x2)	
Bataillons-Stab	
Versorgungszug	2 x light MG34/42
Grenadier-Kompanie (x3)	9 x light MG
	6 x 7.5cm inf gun, 6 x 8cm mortar
Infanteriegeschutz-Kompanie	5 x light MG, 4 x 7.5cm in gun, 8 x 12cm mortar
Panzerzerstorer-Kompanie	4 x light MG
	54 x Panzerschreck
Regiment Tross	

Grenadier-Regiment 1945

Grenadier-Regiment, 1945
Regiments-Stab
Stabs-Kompanie   10 x light MG

Grenadier-Bataillon (x2)
Bataillons-Stab
Versorgungszug   2 x light MG
Grenadier-Kompanie (x3   9 x light MG
Schwere Kompanie   1 x light MG, 8 heavy MG,
5 x light MG, 2 x 15cm inf gun, 8 x 12cm mortar

Panzerzerstorer-Kompanie   4 x light MG, 54 x Panzerschreck (+ 18 in reserve)

Regiments Tross